Brain Fugue
Claire Trévien

VERVE
POETRY PRESS
BIRMINGHAM

PUBLISHED BY VERVE POETRY PRESS
Birmingham, West Midlands, UK
www.vervepoetrypress.com
mail@vervepoetrypress.com

All rights reserved
© 2019 Claire Trévien

The right of Claire Trévien to be identified as author of this work has been asserted in accordance with section 77 of the Copyright, Designs and Patents Act 1988.

No part of this work may be reproduced, stored or transmitted in any form or by any means, graphic, electronic, recorded or mechanical, without the prior written permission of the publisher.

FIRST PUBLISHED FEB 2019

Printed in Birmingham by Positive Print

ISBN: 978-1-912565-15-3

CONTENTS

Sick or Sad?	4
Flâneuse Brain	6
The Brain at Home	7
Brain as Forest	8
Pigeon Brained	12
Broker Brain	18
Shrined Brain	22
Daytime Drinking Brain	23
Brain as Museum	25
Brain Freeze	28
Brains Hard as Hares	29
School for Brains	30
Spider Brain	32
Brain as City	33
House of Brains	35
Storm Brain	36
Orchid Brain	37
Bubbly Brain	38
Code-Switching Brain	39
Brain Fugue	40
Air-Brained	41
Ouija Brain	42
More of a Comment Than a Question Brain	43
Esc Delete Uninstall	44
Acknowledgements	

Sick or Sad?

Since we cannot speak of the landscape of the crowd,
       how it turns from hot to cold in a blink,
       drains my veins dry, makes my body a ghost of itself,
you ask me if my absence was due to being 'sick or sad'?

I use the euphemism 'not well' to blanket over the trees,
       the hills, the path that stops being a path, the carpet
       of burned leaves catching the wheels of trains,
the snow duvet that protects the flowers, or kills them
       (I can never remember which it is).

My sadness is sick, my sickness is sad.
       My sadness has been unplugged from triggers
       you could relate to and lives in a different city now.
       My sickness is so connected to my sadness that I cannot
       tell you which is the chicken, which is the egg.

Here is an ankle sprained after it gave
way on a flat surface like plastic lit by a lighter.
See how it sent my sadness flying and cracked its screen.
       Here is my stomach full of rams fighting about fleeing.

Flâneuse Brain

walking as a body submerging itself in another body   as light refraction
walking as soggy pages   as steeping   as a precious waste of resources

walking as the act of waiting   for your receptacle   to fill
walking as a locked door   a bathbomb drop   all release

how much walking is too much walking   as looking for light damage
the eyes rolling back on themselves   a disbelief in colour

walking as a body out of scale   the vertiginous act of swallowing yourself
it happens   then what   is the distortion

walking as a battery drained before its time   the leap from 44%
to nothing   legs full of networks   but no plugs

when is the walking completed   have you uploaded necessary data
is there a backup folder   are you the backup folder

The Brain at Home

the street has been framed with onyx
the street sits in the bathroom

the headlights dim when you flush
refocus when you dab your
brush with cream

we do not know where
the street was bought
it has always lived here

martha tried to draw on the
street, but her hand

the bathroom has been framed with smoke
the bathroom sits at the crossroads

the tap opens when the lights change a
gush of expletives quieting to a dribble
when the last shoe leaves the road

it is best
to ignore the weather
in the bathroom

cab drivers that fish
tailed into the frame

returned years later
scaled purple

Brain as Forest

The collective noun for tree isn't forest, it's a flooding.

A flooding of trees. You are swimming through our glas,
        the blue-green trees, we are tainting you with each stroke.
Your arms bubble with berries fit to burst.

You've tripped, caught by the swell of a hawthorn,
        your skin turns *glazik*.
I mock you *gwez mor, gwez mor,* the sea of trees.

Your snout is caught in the roots
        where the dead whisper in their busy treacle.
You cannot speak, your belly trapping shadows.

It's true, you are drowning, your face framed in poplar.
        The waves root through your limbs,
twigs spidering up your legs.

A clearing, and I speak: "It's nice that you think I need rescuing".

Your teeth are flowering now
        where is your alphabet? your brain slithers
with *drez, balan, brug, tann, hogan*:

you are spelling MOUTH with brambles,
        broom, heather, sessile oak, hawthorn.
Your tongue is teeming with insects,

skin shedding from your body into keys,
        winged fruit, acorns. One palm torsades
up to the sky as if to palp the clouds.

What are you now but the sound
        of coins pouring down a chute,
strings of ivy plucked and unplucked.

You are foreign in a forest of foreigners,
        your skin is full of our words,
with a new letter, *kerzhin*, added to our alphabet.

Pigeon Brained

It was that time of night when my brain speaks French
but my tongue spews wine, and the weather speaks emoji,
but the streets speak Latin, and my phone is speckled
with the language of my body leaning on it unlocked.

>   Perhaps I'm lucky to live between two languages
>   never needing to get too comfortable with either
>   – which one would I rather dream in?
>   which one swears the best? Do I sweat French?

And I swayed towards home, half-hero half-blurred,
stomping with each step on another seam, one operation
after another stabbed with wild weeds. Considered my body
and its habit of sprouting bruises and cuts during sleep

>   how they themselves journeyed through DNA
>   from ancestors also prone to bruising without
>   need for obstinate furniture. Each a careful
>   operation leading to this very moment

when I find myself stumbling back, the asphalt
bubbling under me, revealing how here – the surface
flakes past pain, allows a shoal to bare its back,
unroll fish scales beneath my feet, swimming somewhere new.

Broker Brain

Ok Claire, understood. I am afraid that in underwriting eyes –
they will not like that. It will alarm them. Your sentences
have no gravity. Narratives barely settle on your words
before flying off again. It does not 'aid' your case for finance.

I see you are French then. That's a bit unfortunate for you.
It helps explain why they observe you from the top of pine
trees. Your sentences clash with your finances. Stop striding,
start saving. I understand your situation, you are your mother,

all of your tabs are open and you don't know how to close them.
If there is something out of the norm involved, I will stop holding on.
Holding on is an important milestone on the way towards an approval.
Not 'my' approval you understand, 'an' approval.

Continue with all the other aspects I have outlined,
as quickly as possible in your own interests
before the narratives fly back down
and impose a horrific order on you.

Shrined Brain

She built unopened homes
across my brain –
>planted these bird feeders
>along the roads, the rush-hour
>avenues, the slow cycle lanes,
>and the unlit alleyways;

there is 1 of me
and 600,000 homes
– shrines to love.
>I say they do not exist
>when the roads tangle into one.
>How am I meant to spot a home
>in the debris of tarmac?

But I know, I can't quite forget
about the smallest one
that ticks away
in its cage of bones.

Daytime Drinking Brain

I hope it doesn't end up   [end]
in one of your poems,   [your poems]
he says.   [he says]
Give me a coaster   [give me]
and I will create   [I will create]
strange confetti, a dagger.   [a dagger]
Rape is so cliché.   [so cliché]
Oh I had a bad experience   [experience]
and now it fills all my words   [my words]
with paralysis and smoke   [smoke]
and *the trauma of it*   [of it]
Yes, I agree, quite enough   [quite enough]
already from other...   [from others]
The pub is intricate like   [like]
a chocolate box – and   [a box]
just as lacquered   [lacking]
and you came back   [and]
wrong.   [wrong]

Brain as Museum

After Clive Birnie

Nothing thrown out, simply rotated
and stored. Today I present the 1998 collection,
curated by an unfortunate encounter with my family.
It'll stay open for a few months until
I quietly retire it to the stockroom.

One day the collection is there, another
it has vanished, replaced by an already sold-out exhibit.
It's as if last season had never happened.

Each day, in tiny ways, the rooms expand big
as a stone dropped in a pond, as deep
as a shell groused in grains.

It's got labels screeched so hard into paper
the pen's pierced through. Do not look down,
there are more on the ground, with the names
of artists I don't recognise, and a bonfire out
back of the ones I've disowned.

Bring your own headphones. Avoid
the gift shop and its small Eiffel towers.

Brain freeze

Putting my hands on the wheel, lights on,
empty road, red evening, ease the gas
and park, handbrake up, body cranked shut,
your bellybutton boxing you to the seat.

Two options before you: the bar to beat
your insides with booze, the sea to switch
your outsides with ice. Or this cold container
of a car, with this body that cannot find
the right levers to move, to drive, to way.

Brains Hard as Hares

Say I strayed
too near the pylons;
that my footprint lacks
an empty slot

and that the dolmens sit too close for comfort.

Say that nature is impermeably green,
a sound barrier gathering momentum.

The drone of crickets
clogs my throat,
the path seems narrower
each time I talk.

This is a tune I have forgotten,
almost,
talking down your arteries,
to that mythical heart.

Say that I've flat-footed my way through this path
one impaired pair of arches to another.

Say this opening is unhollow, say it is an opening,
say open, say low.

School for Brains

After Dorianne Laux

A niggle is their debut.
Eyes pushing at the back of teeth
before true sight.

What is sight but a wooden cube
you read with your gums?

They train the connection
on flesh, the corners of ceilings, and later,
the pile of dust behind the door.

They are told to harden their granite shelter,
decorate their veins with pale green lichen.
Stone brains. Salt brains. Softening brains.

To each their specialty, hunger brains
sun at some saps for days,
coating their surface with biscuit crumbs.

Soon the brains learn to endure
hanging like beads from a tree

Compost brain - one weed
shakes its stems at you,
a flash of future in the dark.

Spider Brain

You, forgotten footnote, running across the page.
A monochromatic huddle in the corner of my brain.

Nothing to see here but your veils, your backspaces,
"it was just here" I tell everyone, and they shudder.

Your legs are taxes I've forgotten to return.
You dance like rusty scissors, moving closer.

I know I will look up in the night soon and see
that leathered parachute poised for descent.

Brain as City

As the sky drawstrings to darkness,
    your buildings wake
– raise their skirts out of the gutter
    with an unsteady focus;
the park uproots itself,
    swings to the right,
its eyes two horses on springs,
    its mouth of sand empties.
The river abandons her bed
    tips out into the street,
(which itself has unlocked its jaws,
    the crossroad crumples into
the alley, headlines procreate
    with street signs, "STOP CHICKEN",
"ORGANIC KING", "WARNINGLAND").
    Now, the Ladbrokes rolls out
like a rubber band ball,
    accumulating house numbers.
They lurch forward: bus stops,
    compost bins, roofs of clay, slate, and grit,
doors united into a leg
    (windows leave
the most curious prints behind),
    and they sink deep, and then deeper,
into the mushrooming ground,
    not a spire left
to periscope.

House of Brains

A home is a door you can unlock.
        A brain is a balloon full of glow-worms.
        It is an invertebrate substance you can't shake too hard.

My home this month has been my father's garage,
converted so that there is a bed instead of a car.
        The previous owners baptised the garage Ti Nay,
        meaning House of the Fool, House of the Idiot, House of the Mad.

Each night I unlock doors wide enough for four wheels
and drive my brain inside.
        I could only hope for Ti Mad which I would translate
        as House of the Good and not House of the Broken.

When there is no storm, I am reminded that my brain is ungrounded.
        I see mad everywhere, selling me biscuits and sweets,
        everything is good, and mad, and full of crumbs.

That it tends to get stuck against the ceiling
buoyed by too much helium and self-preservation.
        I choose to translate Ti Nay as House of the Trusting.
        I trust myself through its mouth every night.

Tonight will have other tonights.

Storm Brain

You rush out as the buzzing intensifies,
somewhere above you is a net of lightning.
A wreck of wasps falls from the sky,
unnerves your car. Your eyelids can't
swipe fast enough, before wave after wave
relentlessly pours over your face,
empties your stomach out in jolts
of electricity. Stay away from the windows.
Unplug anything with a screen blinking
time, words, or images at you.

Orchid Brain

        I Google "How not to kill you"
      and am faced
      with incantations I need
      to do another shop for.
     Show
    me
   sur-
  vi
  val.
  Does
 it
 do
 door-
 to-
 door
 de
 live
 ry?
I water it every day until
the roots are drowning.
Starve it. Keep it in the pot
until it's outgrown.

Bubbly Brain

'je bois des étoiles' Dom Pérignon

I am a minor laughter widow,
an act of vandalism founded
this afternoon.

All our families are equally old,
but some know how to pick up
their barrels and dance.

To avoid exploding with laughter
keep yourself in complete darkness,
undisturbed, and at a steady temperature.

Put your laughter in a cupboard
that is seldom opened,
or under a bed that is seldom used.

There is, of course, the problem
of exploding bottles,
and my notebook has been shaken.

Code-Switching Brain

"We develop awareness of when to 'code-switch': to move back and forth between two languages" - Hanan Ben Nafa

We start off in one lane, eyes on rear-view,
develop arms to switch gears better, increase
awareness of obstacles, of figures in darkness,
of squirrels dashing before our sentences.

When the lights turn red, we pause, unsure of
tongue shapes, something as simple as 'oh' a
code too tough to crack. How is the 'O' formed?
Switch on, lights green, and the engine takes over.

To drive is automatic, but sometimes you glitch:
"move along!" (it is a kite not a car), and then
back: you are again driving the wrong vehicle
and your other rules do not apply here. (and so

forth). And then, it's hard to resist driving a kite:
between the strings you see a road developing
two borders carpeting behind you comically, their
languages booming and then seceding to light.

Brain Fugue

My first fugue was aged 4. My last is yet to come.

- My brain walked me to our neighbours and asked them to adopt me. My sisters collected me, swore I was fine.
- I don't remember my second or third fugue.
- The fugues I don't remember are more successful.
- I cottoned on that a fugue necessitates a handkerchief tied to a stick.
- A handkerchief cannot hold much on the end of a stick.

I walked over the rocks until the sea stopped me, then returned.

- Writing adieux can be an effective way to prevent a fugue.

Later, I accumulated objects for homes I'd never settle in.

- Then, I fugued from the boxes.
- The buildings tried to hug me, and I ducked out of their arms.

My relationships became purely digital.

- My body grew more layers to keep it still.
- My brain outgrew the pain in my body. It observed me from the ceiling.

My in-built satnav tells me when it's time to turn left.

- Run before they abandon you.
- Run before they take your spirit.
- Run before the red flags turn bloody.

Air Brained

1. My memories have vanished, I tug at them, expecting the resistance of roots, but there is nothing.
2. Nothing is never nothing. The polluted air says the city is not open. though the pavements breathe better than I do.
3. My questions are sending questions to each other to pass the time.
4. Nothing is a terror that cannot be described because it is nothing. Your brain has masses of nothing floating too far to reach. I can tell you this one is cold, but not its contents.
5. Nothing makes it impossible to concentrate.
6. A memory buzzes to life as if on the telly in the neighbour's flat, but I close the curtains and ignore it.
7. Nothing isn't uncomfortable.
8. Some types of air are easier to contain than others. I appear to be very easy to contain.
9. I begin an inventory of my brain: moss, yellow, a cork keyring, a chipped ceiling...
10. A chipped ceiling.
11. I abandon the inventory. Nothing can't be distorted.
12. I know that I cannot trust the air.
13. The television has turned back on, but I cannot tell what it is showing me.
14. The air is turning to water, it has extracted the drops air was so carefully dissimulating.
15. My brain is filling with a substance heavier than nothing. Water sloshes against my forehead, makes my neck bend with the effort.
16. Water-brained is not so different from air-brained, except it is more tiring to stay in one place.

17. I want you to know, if you are reading this, that I am trying to drain the water.
18. Let me rephrase that: the water will drain itself when it is ready to.
19. The cattle grid descends, sifts through the bubbles of air, divides the brain into two stagnant pools.
20. Did you know brain-bubbles could be static? They stick to one another to insulate the brain.
21. I dream of waking in a glorious mess, weeds and bugs and viruses, a muddy handprint on the wall of my brain.

Ouija Brain

Not a yes, that would be to a different question. One to which no
      Backyard BBQ
notice is required. We lower our hands, salmon-flushed, on the board.
      Cakes from our Patisserie
Noises of noses at our throat, snuffling us out. No
      Fresh-produce homemade
nod, we are frozen, but the word bubbles chant-like in our brain
      We will craft your favourite tipple
now. There are no letters or numbers on the board but a swell.
      Simplicity & Freshness
Notes low in register are lifted from the well. You are a
      Pomegranate passion fruit flavours
novice to evasion dear volcano, but it just takes one domino to
      Drink beer it is good for you
non-stand for all to fall, a succession of dots before a crash.
      It's easy & tastes so much better

More of a Comment Than a Question Brain

```
i ha           ve turned
on      the                        tap
s             & can        not
close    the   m    with the
se            so    apy       ha
n          d     s
```

Esc Delete Uninstall

My brain's installed a decoder
that translates everything told to me into
"I wish you were dead".
"Pass the butter", "What time
is your train", "I can't make
it tonight" all mean, "I wish
you were dead". When my sister
asks me to drive her children, she wishes
I were dead. When my mother asks
me to make her phone work,
she wishes I were dead. The person
at the post office stopped smiling
briefly as she tapped on the till. She too,
wishes I were dead. I do not wish
to be dead, but peer pressure is a bitch.

I throw my hands into the static to find
the real the what the tape I twist
the neck of the make the butter
phrase book phase a right hook
nope some glimmer that looks
like truth is there shapeshifting
from hate to love and back again.

ABOUT THE AUTHOR:

Claire Trévien is a British-Breton writer currently living in Brittany, France. She is the author and editor of several poetry and non-fiction books including The Shipwrecked House, which was longlisted in the Guardian First Book Award. She was the recipient of a Hawthornden Castle Fellowship in 2018. Trévien founded Sabotage Reviews and now runs site-specific creative writing retreats. For more information visit clairetrevien.co.uk

BY THE SAME AUTHOR:

Low-Tide Lottery (Salt, 2011)
The Shipwrecked House (Penned In The Margins, 2013)
Astéronymes (Penned In The Margins, 2016)

ACKNOWLEDGEMENTS:

With thanks to the following competitions, publishers and curators. 'Brain as City' won 3rd prize in the Verve Poetry Festival Competition and was published in its anthology It *All Radiates Outward* (Verve Poetry Press, 2018). A version of 'Pigeon Brained' was highly commended in the Live Cannon Poetry Competition and published in its anthology. 'Brain Fugue' and 'Daytime Drinking Brain' both featured in *The Dizziness of Freedom* anthology (Bad Betty Press, 2018). 'Code-switching brain' and 'Pigeon Brained' appeared in the *Wretched Strangers* anthology (Boiler House Press, 2018) with slightly different titles. A version of 'Brain as Forest' was performed on BBC3's The Verb on 19th October 2018 with Kate Arnold's music.

I am grateful to Hawthornden Castle Fellowship for giving me the space to finish this pamphlet.